AF655233

For Sara, Jackie and Kate

Acknowledgements

A special "Thank You" to the thousands of people who have been part of the audiences in my hundreds of live seminars. Your participation and feedback continues to impact my writing and speaking career. You have all helped make me a better person.

Special thanks to my father-in-law, Bob Phelan. His decades as a language teacher and his proofing skills continue to help me with the written word.

NETWORKING Simplified

From his award-winning
90 minute seminar presentation

Thom Singer

MANJUL

Manjul Publishing House

First published in India by

MANJUL

Manjul Publishing House Pvt. Ltd.

Corporate Office:

2nd Floor, Usha Preet Complex,

42 Malviya Nagar, Bhopal 462 003 - India

E-mail: manjul@manjulindia.com Website: www.manjulindia.com

Sales & Marketing Office:

7/32, Ground Floor, Ansari Road, Daryaganj, New Delhi 110 002

Email: sales@manjulindia.com

Thom Singer asserts the moral right to be identified
as the author of this work.

Originally published as *Networking Unplugged*
by *Thom Singer*

Published by arrangement with New Year Publishing, LLC

Copyright © 2009 by New Year Publishing, LLC

This edition first published in India in 2013

ISBN 978-81-8322-360-7

Printed & bound in India by Thomson Press (India) Ltd.

All rights reserved. No part of this publication may be reproduced, stored in or introduced into a retrieval system, or transmitted, in any form, or by any means (electronic, mechanical, photocopying, recording or otherwise) without the prior written permission of the publisher. Any person who does any unauthorized act in relation to this publication may be liable to criminal prosecution and civil claims for damages.

Contents

This book is a transcription of my live presentation "Some Assembly Required: How to Make, Grow and Keep Your Business Relationships." While the presentation is customized and changes with each audience, this is a good overview.

Introduction

Thank you all for being here. Hopefully you'll find this presentation to be informative, entertaining, *and* interactive. If I say something during the course of the presentation and you think, "Hey, I agree. That's exactly how my company, my team, or I do that," go ahead and raise your hand. Jump in. Share your experiences. We'll add your story to the mix. If I say something with which you disagree, I want to hear that as well. I want to hear from you as the presentation progresses, how all this information applies to your professional, and personal life.

I wrote a book called *Some Assembly Required—How to Make, Grow and Keep Your Business Relationships*. My background includes being active in sales and marketing roles for large companies for over 17 years. One of the things I've experienced is that *people do business with people that they know, like, and trust*. My career was made by opportunities that were brought to me by people that I met through an active focus on networking. Networking is not just about meeting people and trading business cards, but instead it is about creating mutually beneficial long-term relationships. I had the opportunity to write my books and create several presentations, speaking to audiences all over the country, because of the people in my network. This is what I'm here to share with you.

One of the many things I have observed in the business world is that your clients and your customers have many choices, and business is getting more complicated. The business community is getting more competitive than it has ever been, no matter in what industry you work. Everywhere you go, you and your clients are faced with choices.

Too Many Choices

When you go into Starbuck's, immediately when you walk up to the bar you have 19,000 choices that you can make at that exact moment in which you order your beverage. That is because of the different sizes they offer, regular, decaf, and all the different flavors they brew every day. Then you get to the specialty drinks with all the flavored syrups. You look at the non-coffee drinks, all the different cold, hot, and frozen things that they serve, coffees, waters, sodas, teas, Frappuccinos, etc.... It is overwhelming. But every time that I walk into a Starbuck's, I order a Grande Non-fat Vanilla Latte. Every time! Why do I do that? Because I know the Grande Vanilla Latte. I like the Grande Vanilla Latte. It's my morning friend. It's my choice because I'm comfortable with it.

And that happens in business. When people are making a decision, they'll bring two or three companies in and let them make presentations and submit proposals, but very often, they make their decision based on what they already know.

They select the vendor with whom they are most comfortable, and this is often the one they have already known the longest.

It is the same thing with cookies! I will share a secret with you—I love Oreo cookies. But Oreos now come in 19 different flavors and colors. I always thought Oreos were chocolate cookies with white cream filling. But they come in mint and mocha and other flavors. At the holidays they are created in different colors—they come in green for St. Patrick's Day, orange for Halloween, red, white, and blue for the 4th of July. Red and green at Christmas. I was giving this speech not too long ago and somebody tossed a bag of mini Oreos at me from the snacks that they had at the table. They were the size of a nickel. They also make larger ones. So now you can't just go buy Oreos. Now you have to make another choice. I like it simple. If I am going to be real crazy I might buy the "Double Stuff"—but I don't need 19 choices of Oreos!

Competition and choices are everywhere and it's not going to go away, no matter in what industry you're working. So you have to build a network to help you cut through the clutter. But to build that network takes a commitment of time. And one of the things people say is, "Hey, I've got to sell to today's customers. I don't have time to go to conferences. I don't have time to meet new people. I already have enough friends. I've got too much to do with the clients, prospects, and other people who are already in my life."

I'm not saying you should stop doing your current work, because that's very important. You have to meet your current sales quota. You have to meet your current job requirements. You have to serve those clients you're already working with. But an investment in your network is an investment in the future. It is your future revenue source. It is your safety net for the rough times.

Nobody Can Network For You

I speak often at law firms, because I used to work in that field. One of the things I ask lawyers is, "How many of your current clients today—your three top-billing clients—are the same top three that you were working with three years ago, or five years ago?" The answer is almost always, "zero." Sure, there are some who have a unique practice that continues to serve the same clients year after year, but in most cases they have a constant flow of new clients. My next question is, "Who're going to be your clients in three more years?" They don't know. And if they're not out there looking to fill a pipeline with potential clients and referral sources, they may not *have* clients in a few years.

The other thing about networking is that nobody can do this for you. You can't ask your assistant to go out and build your reputation in the business community. You can't ask your husband or wife to join charity boards or industry associations, or to write articles for you. You can't have someone else go build your reputation. That's why I call my presentation and my books "Some Assembly Required"—because you have to put the pieces together. It is like on Christmas morning when the kid runs down the steps and sees that shiny new bicycle. Someone had to put it together, often mom or dad late the night before. A frame, some handle bars, a chain, two tires, and a seat spread around the living room would not have the same impact.

Why Network?

So why would you do this networking stuff? This is a big commitment. You already have a job that demands a lot of time, you already have a family, and you already have other interests. Why would you take on more to do on purpose? Well, for most of you in this room, your career requires you to develop new business. Your job is to make sure that more revenues are coming into the company. I started this whole thing off by saying people are going to do business with people that they know, like, and trust. Over and over again, people are going to use their minds to research your product or service. But in the end, they're going to use that gut instinct and say, "I just feel there's something about 'Dave.' I really trust he's going to come through for me on this deal."

Many times when you have clients, they look to you as sort of their trusted advisor on any subject that relates to what you do for a living. But then they may come to you and ask you questions that are way outside of your area of expertise. When that happens, you've got three choices.

1. You can look at them and say, "That is not what I do. I don't know." Well, you haven't really helped your client and probably haven't advanced your position with them.

2. You could lie to them; you could just make something up. But that's going to come back to bite you. You don't want that to happen. You will harm your reputation and probably get fired.

3. But the third thing you can do is say, "You know, that's not my area of expertise. But I know someone, and that is what they do. Let me introduce you to them." What you've done is you've just put two people in your network together. And usually they're thrilled that you've done that and they'll look for ways to repay that favor to you.

It also strengthens the visibility of your company. Companies spend a lot of money on marketing and ads and all kinds of great things, and those who work for the organization feel that there are other people who handle the "visibility part." They think, "Well we have ads, thus people know who we are." But people have become suspect of advertising, and there is always more of a bond when they know real people who are part of the organization. Besides, if you're not out on the streets, face-to-face with customers, maybe your competitors are there establishing the friendships that will influence future buying decisions. Out of sight is out of mind. It doesn't matter how many TV commercials your company runs, if they're sitting next to your competitor at an industry conference talking to them on a personal level, that is the real deal. You have to be out there adding to the visibility.

And finally, networking helps you further your career. All opportunities come from people. If you want others to think of you when they need to buy your product or service ... or if you want to hear about the great job opportunity or promotion, you have to make sure that you are on their mind.

There may be some other job you want, either inside or outside your company. Thus it is important that others know you and know about your goals.

People say to me all the time when I talk about networking that I'm just pushing visibility, that I'm positioning networking as if it's more important than all other aspects of business. They try to point out that their business is all about credibility—not visibility. But I'm not doing that. I think both are necessary—and it's not a competition. Both are important. It's important that your company has a good reputation and that you, individually, have that good reputation. However, everybody claims credibility. Every single one of your competitors goes in to make a presentation with a great PowerPoint, great brochures, a great list of references, and they go in verbalizing that their product is superior. You might think that yours is superior, and it might be, but it's confusing to the client because everybody is coming in with statistics and studies and third-party research, saying that their product or service is the best. So the decision makers are confused.

I like this analogy. Say you're in New York City and you're looking for a tall building, a 45-story building. You're standing on a sidewalk and you're looking up. There's a 50-story building, a 55-story building. You can't tell which one is taller from the sidewalk. And you know what? It really doesn't matter to you because your need is a 45-story building, so either one is fine for your purposes.

When I use this analogy some retort with, "Well, you don't understand industry. My clients are sophisticated. They're up in a helicopter. They're flying around high in the air and they know which is better."

Maybe. Maybe not. But I argue that most decision makers aren't that sophisticated. And a lot of them are down on that sidewalk, and even though they might know a lot, they're still looking up saying,

"Wow, they both look good to me. And either one will meet my needs." So it has to come back to that intangible feeling that you're bringing forth as a human being relating to other people—and it's going to make that difference in their buying decision.

Plus, if nobody knows you exist, you're not going to get invited to the table anyway. Don't confuse the two. Realize that I'm talking about a balance. You have to have both. You have to have both visibility and the credibility.

Face to Face Networking

So let's talk about networking in the context of going to a business event where you're going to be interacting with people. There are a lot of common mistakes that we all make when we go out to these types of events. Number one: people don't treat everybody they meet with respect. They meet somebody and maybe they're with a company that they don't like, or they've had a bad experience with someone else from that company. Or maybe that person's title isn't high enough up the organization chart, or maybe it's on the wrong side of business. Thus they blow the person off. And the person might want to talk to them and they're like, "Whatever." People have very long memories. If you fail to treat someone with respect, it might be years later when they're sitting across from you and you're trying to sell them—you might not even remember them—but you'd be surprised how many people remember you five, ten years later, if you were rude. So you always want to make sure that you treat everybody with respect.

Another thing about networking is that it takes more than one or two encounters to have somebody actually be part of your network. If we met tonight, that doesn't make you part of my network. It makes you someone I just met. There is a big difference between someone you have met and someone with whom you have established a long-term, mutually beneficial friendship. So, it's a continuous thing. It's not just, "Hey, I'm going to go out to one or two events, and meet one or two people, and my phone's going to ring off the hook." This is an ongoing process that is always part of your business life.

Oftentimes, people will show up late to business events. They see in the program, oh it starts at 5:30, but the speaker goes on at 6:00. So they assume it is great to show up at 6:05. And then, right around 7:00, when the speaker starts taking questions from the audience the person will sneak out that back door. Their excuse for running out early is usually something about "beating the traffic out of the parking lot."

The next day when they are back at the office their boss might ask, "Hey, did you go to that networking function?" They'll say, "Oh, yeah, sir, I went." NO THEY DIDN'T. They were there, but they were not networking. What they really did was spend $20, $30, $40, $100 of the company's money—whatever it costs to be there—to eat a substandard hotel dinner and to sneak out the back door without talking to anyone. The part about meeting people, the actual part of building your reputation and building connections with other people, happens before the speaker and after the speaker. Professional speakers are really nice people and have entertaining programs, but listening to someone talk is NOT networking. You have to actively seek out others and ask questions of them to discover the power of creating business relationships.

When you are talking to people at a business event, be engaged in the moment. How many of you have ever had this happen? You're at an event. You meet somebody. When they're talking to you, they're sort of looking over your shoulder, trying to find someone else whom they might talk with instead of you. If you're going to talk with someone, be present in the conversation with that person. Even if it's someone that you really don't want to talk to or you don't feel that you're going to be able to build a long-term relationship with, even if there's no type of connection that's going to be beneficial. You still need to be polite. Don't look past them and not listen to what they are saying. While you are not going to want to talk for long periods of time with everyone, and sometimes you will not like a person, you still must show respect. It's a skill to learn how to get out of a conversation when you're kind of trapped with somebody. You need to be conscious of your body language and the words you use to excuse yourself, lest you be seen as a jerk.

Business Cards

How many of you have business cards on you right now? You always need to have business cards on you, even when you're coming to an event inside your own company. Always have business cards on you wherever you go, because you never know when you're going to meet somebody that you might have that connection with. You want to make sure you have the opportunity to follow up with each other, and a business card is a great business tool.

Some trivialize this, but business cards are really important. They contain vital information about a person and they make follow-up much easier. A card is considered a standard tool for networking. It is a socially acceptable thing when you're having a conversation, to say, "Hey, do you have a card?" If you're going to ask for theirs, you should be able to produce yours. Otherwise you may appear to be a self-centered taker. "Hey, do you have a card? Oh, I don't. I don't want to give you my information, but I want yours later because I want to try to sell something to you. However I have no intention of letting you contact me." But if you're able to produce your card, say, "Oh, do you have a card? I'd like to follow up with you sometime." It's an equal exchange. And if you don't have a card, sometimes people look at you like, "What, aren't you prepared?"

I spoke at a company once where their senior team told me, "We actually never bring cards with us as a corporate policy." I asked, "Why?" They responded, "Because when we meet people, we can say oh no, I don't have a card, but if you give me yours, I'll follow up with you. Now we have a reason to follow up." I inquired if they always followed up … EVERY TIME? Because if not, then you are lying to people and showing that you are not one who keeps your word. You never want your first meeting with people to convey that you are unprepared, lying, or not interested in them. It's easier if you just always have cards that you can exchange.

And then the most important of all of these things, the biggest mistake that people make, is not following up with people they meet. We all meet fabulous people all the time who could be very good referral sources, clients, future co-workers, or friends. But after meeting them we don't do anything about it. We take their card and it ends up getting lost.

Easy Steps to Connect

But there are some easy things that you can do when you're going to a networking event, and those include making it a point that when you walk into a room you tell yourself, "I'm going to meet three to five new people." Every time! Now, five is a number that I use. If you're not that outgoing in a social situation, maybe you pick three. If you're real gung-ho, you pick seven. But, have a number and make it a point to try and meet the new people every single time you put yourself into a social business situation.

The other thing is don't stand around or sit with people from your company. Take the initiative to make sure that you're talking to other people. And if you're at an event where it's not assigned seating, try to split up from co-workers and go to different tables. Sometimes your company has bought a table and you have to sit together. But if you're at an event where it's not assigned seating, if five of you from your organization sit at five different tables of ten, combined you could meet 45 people. If you're at an industry conference, and your boss has invested the money to send five people to the event, you should make it a priority to meet as many people as you can. What are the odds that 1 out of 45 could be someone your company could do business with? Pretty good. If you all sit at the same table, combined you can only meet five people. You do the math!

You also should try to look for people you've met before, because meeting someone once or twice doesn't make them part of your network. So you want to look for people you've already met so that you can talk to them a little bit more and set another brick in that foundation of your relationship with them. In addition, when you speak with people you know, they will most likely introduce you to others, and then it helps you with your goal of meeting three to five new people.

If you're going to be talking to somebody, be engaged, be interested in the conversation. Ask them questions about their life. Often, people will get into a situation and they'll meet someone who could be the dream client. They've been trying to get into this company forever and they pounce on the person they just met right there in the middle of a networking event. Immediately they're saying, "Hey, I work for Company X and we do this and that and we can provide this solution for your company." Their focus is all about me, me, me, me, I, I, this is what we can do, we can do, we can do. Well, people don't want that the moment they meet you. They care more about themselves than they do about you. Give them a chance to talk about themselves first. They want you to ask questions and learn about them before you tell them how great you are. I try not to go into a selling situation the first time I meet somebody. I try to find out more about them, ask them questions about their lives. But many people, including me, struggle with fighting the urge to just talk about themselves. Be honest with yourself and work on having a set of questions you can ask others before you talk about yourself.

I know a person who consults with marketing and sales teams. And one thing he does is looks at sales letters and introductory emails with a red pen and a blue pen in hand. Every time he finds the words "I," "we," or "our solution," he circles them in red. And every time the company talks about the client using the words "you," "your benefit," or "your advantages," he circles in blue. He says, without question, most of the time those pages are 4 to 1 red to blue. And he hands them back to his clients and says, "Make it the other way." When you're interacting with people, you want to try to get them to talk four times more than you do. You want to be asking them four questions for every answer you're giving. Now, if you run into someone else who's really good at this, it's going to be 50/50 because they're going to be asking you questions, and you're going to be asking them questions. But most of the time, you're not going to run into people who have trained in networking and trained in asking questions. So if you're asking questions, you're going to get them to open up and talk and tell you about their lives so that you can find some areas of common ground.

Remember, whenever you are talking with people, always have something positive to say. So often we can have a bad day at work, a boss can be on our case, or we're not meeting quota—whatever it is. And someone says, "Hey, how are things at your job?" And people reply, "Oh, man. It stinks. The boss is on my case." Or some other diatribe that laments all the problems in their world. Save that for your spouse or your therapist. All this person who doesn't know you hears is "blah, blah, blah, bad, bad, bad, blah, blah, blah, bad, bad, bad." Later on, what happens to them is a buying situation comes up, and they don't even know why, but they just have a bad feeling about you or your company. They may tell others. Rumors fly that maybe it's not a good place to work; maybe there's drama going on. Thus you should always have positive things to say about your work environment. Don't tell tales out of school. If things aren't great, don't be the person who's going out telling other people in the industry. Just have something positive to say or say nothing at all. Even if it's bad, just say, "You know, I work with a real dynamic group of people. It gets better every day." And change the subject. Not that any of you would ever have a bad day—but be conscious of the fact that if you let the negative stuff fly off your tongue you are setting your reputation up as that of one who always has a black cloud following them.

Whenever you attend a business event sponsored by an organization, remember that a person is behind the planning of the event. Get involved. Volunteer to help. One of the hardest things for organizers is getting people to work the check-in table or assist with other details. One of the hardest things is getting people to be on the committee to plan these events. Be the person who says, "Hey, I'll help." Lots of times companies will volunteer people in their organization. And you know, if you have people working the different parts of the events, other companies see that and they'll say, "They're everywhere."

People often ask me about where to find the best organizations for networking. They don't know where to start. My simple answer is that business professionals are everywhere, and you can meet people at a variety of different types of events. You just have to look. There are hundreds of business events, corporate seminars, industry training classes, trade shows, happy hour mixers, cultural events, sporting events, and other gatherings that draw professionals to attend. There are places where you go for fun; there are places like your church or your synagogue; there's your neighborhood. And if you can't find an event where the right types of business people are, create your own. Reach into your Rolodex and say, "Hey whom do I know? I'm going to invite ten people just to meet for happy hour and I'm going to ask them to bring one or two other people in the industry." Creating your own events is a great way to meet lots of people and to forge your reputation as someone in your community who can make things happen.

Networking Myths

Everybody has opinions about networking. Some will be positive, some will be indifferent, some might be negative, but everyone I have met has some sort of preset opinion on what we were talking about.

There are a lot of myths that go along with networking, and the first one is that *networking is only for when you're not busy*. "I'm working 50-60 hours a week; I don't have time for any of that." I argue that you have to work it in. It has to be part of your life. Reaping the outstanding benefits from having a strong network does not happen by accident. The most successful people I know are also the most busy. They also are the ones with the most incredible mutually beneficial relationships. They do not ever claim they are "too busy" for other people!

The second myth is that *only the senior people in my company network*. They know all the other senior people in the industry, and they get the business. I don't have to spend my time on networking. Well, maybe. But that doesn't help you personally. I argue that even if you're not the senior person, you want to know people at your level in other companies. Knowing lots of people who are at similar career stages helps you because as you go up the ladder, you sort of grow up in the industry with other people. So by knowing other people when you're younger and you're starting out, someday when you're at that high level, you'll already have a network of peers that have reached those higher levels.

The third myth is that *people you meet never refer you business*. Anybody believe that? I mean, I've gotten so much business in my career from people that I've met in the industries I've worked in, that I don't need to talk about this one. This is not a myth; this one is a lie. People in all types of businesses in cities all over the world get referral business every day. If you really think that nobody ever refers business, you are just wrong.

My favorite myth is the fourth one: *if you're really good, the business will find you*. And that's true. Some business will find you if you have a reputation for doing good work. But if that's all that you rely on, you're leaving a lot of business on the table and I personally would rather have more business than less business. I call this myth the "Kevin Costner School of Doing Business:" "If you build it, they will come." You cannot rely on people knowing how good you are; you have to tell them!

And then there's the fifth myth that *decision makers never attend networking events*. What are they, hermits? Everybody goes somewhere. Everybody goes somewhere besides their home and the office. If you're not finding them, you're just not going to the right type of events and maybe you need to go to different places. But also, you need to not be focused on only meeting decision makers. Meeting any variety of other people inside a company who have access to the decision maker can help you reach the person you want to meet.

One of the greatest examples of connecting with a "non-decision maker" who had access came at a time in my career when I sold to law firms. At one of the biggest firms in my town none of the partners would take my calls. For two or three months, I couldn't get anywhere. But I got to know the marketing manager. She was great. We became friends. One day I told her, "I'm just having the worst time getting to meet any of the partners in your firm." She decided to make it her goal to introduce me to those I needed to meet. We set up a time to go have coffee, but she told me, "Meet at the office; don't meet me at Starbuck's."

So I go up, and this law firm is one of those ones that are like Fort Knox. You cannot get past the receptionist. She stands there with the evil eye, and a determination to not let a vendor anywhere near the attorneys. I ask for Kimberly, and the receptionist instructs me to sit in a chair across the lobby. When Kimberly comes out she gives me a hug and says, "Let's go to Starbuck's." She pushes the elevator button and says, "I don't have my purse. Come on." We walked right past that receptionist. Kimberly took me door-to-door to every partner and every senior associate. I met them all. Now, having met them, I had reason to follow up. They knew who I was; they knew I was Kimberly's friend. I would see them at events; I could talk to them. Over two years, I ended up winning all of that firm's business. It took a while, but it was just getting that first introduction. So, yeah, I couldn't meet the decision makers, but eventually I was able to meet them because I met someone who worked for them.

Know Whom You Want to Meet

Before you go out into these business events, know whom it is that you want to meet. Who are the top ten prospects that you would like to have as clients? Maybe this is an exact company name, or maybe it's just a diagram of what the perfect client looks like. If you don't know whom you want as your client, you won't know if they're sitting right next to you.

Is there anyone who's going to be at one of these events that you want to meet? Do you know in advance that a certain CEO or CIO of a company is going to be at this event? And then who is it that you know who might be able to introduce you? Set it up in advance. Make a phone call to a mutual contact and say, "Hey, I really want to meet your friend Ryan Jones. When we're at this conference, can you find a way to make that meeting happen?" You know what? People will do it for you. People get excited to help you out. You just have to make the effort.

Once you arrive at an event, you go to check-in; you get your nametag. Usually your nametag is going to be pre-printed, so you don't have a lot of control over it. But if maybe they had a printer go down, or you're standing in for someone else, make sure when you fill out your name tag that you write your whole name and your company name legibly. A nametag is a tool, just as we talked about the business card as a tool. If your nametag only reads "Billy" it doesn't allow anyone to start a conversation with you. If it has your full name and your company name someone may say, "Oh, you work for Whole Foods. My sister works for Whole Foods." And now a conversation has started. Make it easy for people to approach you. What you want is to make it as easy as possible for someone to start a conversation with you. So the nametag is an easy way to make you more approachable by those who can read your name and basic information. You want to make sure that you wear it and that it is visible.

If you are uncomfortable in this type of business/ social networking situation then head straight for the food or the bar. And I don't mean to go get liquored up. The reason to head for the food or bar is that it puts you in a line with other people. What happens when you stand in line for the food or the bar is that you are put together with other people. You're standing next to someone and it makes it really easy to start some small talk. You can talk about, "Hey the food looks good." There's always something you can talk about when you're forced into a situation where you're standing next to something. So make the effort. If you're not the type of person who will walk right up to a group and jump into their conversation, finding a way that you get put together with people can make it easier to start that conversation.

Always have your business card with you. One of the tricks to ensure you are never without cards is to keep a stash in your car. Go through your closet and place some in the pockets of your different coats, so that wherever you end up, if you run out of the office, you don't show up and say, "Oh, I don't have business cards." Keep some in your car so you know you have them in the glove compartment. The other day, I showed up at an event in Austin, and I didn't have any business cards. People kidded me because I am the guy who teaches networking skills. It was as if the word had spread that I had no cards, and people were having fun giving me a hard time. They were saying, "Didn't you write a book about this stuff—isn't that part about business cards on page 16 of the book?" People were all over me. What happened was that my wife and I switched cars, I was late, I was running out of the office, and I thought, "I've got a dozen cards in the glove compartment." I get to the event, and suddenly I realize I'm not driving my car. So now I keep business cards in my wife's car, too, so that that will never happen again. I've probably driven her car twice in the last three years, but the next time it happens, I've got extra cards nearby if I need them. Additionally my wife carries some of my cards in her purse so that if I run out when we are out together, I've always got a backup. Find little ways to make sure you're never going to run out of business cards.

And this can be more difficult for women, as your business clothes do not often have pockets like men's suits do. We talk about this, and other tips for women, in my book *Some Assembly Required: A Networking Guide for Women*. Just because you don't have pockets in your suit, does not mean you can skip having cards with you. You just have to discover more creative ways to have access to them.

So what happens if something comes up? You've signed up for a conference or a business dinner and an emergency comes along and you have to change your plans at the last minute. What do you do? Well, our lives are busy. There's a lot of stuff that can pop up and force you to rearrange your calendar. This happens all the time. Your customers come first. There's no doubt about it. You can't say, "I've got to go to the networking event. I can't help you with that problem." No, obviously you have to solve the problem at hand, but you also need to be careful not to send the wrong message to your business community or look unreliable to others who were expecting you to keep your commitment to attend the event.

Begin by trying to send someone else from your company, especially if your company has paid in advance for you to attend. There's nothing that bothers me more than money that's spent, but no one goes to the event. That is just wasted money.

I go to a lot of these events and they cost $50, $60, $100, and you just see all these nametags that aren't picked up. They should have sent somebody else from the company. By sending someone you can get them to pick up your nametag. Because what happens at a lot of these events, especially if you're in kind of a small-knit business community, is people will walk by that nametag table and they'll sort of scan them with their eyes. They want to assess whom will be in attendance. They get there early. They want to get a good look; they want to know who they can seek out to talk with at the event. But on their way out, they go by the nametag table again and they look to see who no-showed. If a lot of people do this, you and your company can start to develop a reputation of being people who always RSVP and never show up.

People don't talk about this stuff, but they just sort of know who in town never seems to follow through on commitments. You might not think that showing up at an event is a commitment, but if you RSVP, it is a way of giving your word that you will attend. Those who regularly no-show can negatively impact their personal brand in the community. I had a friend who really wanted to get on this one charity board. He'd worked really hard to be considered for a spot the next time there was an opening. I helped make sure that his name was put up for consideration. When the board voted on a new member—I found out through one of my friends on the board—his name was brought up and they talked about how he really wanted to participate, how he worked for a great company, and how he'd be a great addition to the board. And then someone else on the board, who's never met him said, "He has a reputation for not showing to stuff. This is a working board. We can't have people who just want to have their name on our letterhead." Somebody else said, "Oh, that's right," and that's when they went on to the next candidate. He has no idea why he didn't get on the board. He thought he'd done everything right. But because of his lack of attention to his networking reputation he was not seen as one who follows through.

If you've been invited to a special event by somebody and then you can't go, call and apologize. Do it because people work hard to put these events on. I know a woman who put together a dinner recently, who had invited two attorneys, two venture capitalists, two accountants, and a banker, to join her for an evening to discuss the local economic conditions affecting their overlapping businesses. She just wanted to pull together some really interesting people to talk about what was going on in the business community. Neither lawyer showed up. She told me later that she went to the rest room at one point and checked her voice mail. One of the lawyers, Micky, had called her and said, "Cheryl, I am so sorry. Something came up. I had an explosion with one of my clients. I tried to get one of my partners, one of the associates, heck, I tried to get our marketing manager to come to your dinner because I know you'd worked hard on it. It just didn't work out. I am sorry." Peter, the other lawyer, never called her. Five weeks later she saw him at an event and asked him about it. He said, "Oh, I got busy." Well the next time she did one of these VIP events, Micky was the first person she invited. She will never invite the other guy. He will never be at her table because he just blew it off. He didn't call to say I'm sorry. Both of them had the same thing happen; they both got busy. That's a fair excuse. But make sure that you take the time to tell other people, "Hey, I'm sorry about that."

Networking is Not a Solo Activity

Who's the best networker? I get asked this question all the time and I take this from a book by a guy named Harvey MacKay, in his book called *Dig Your Well Before You're Thirsty*. He says, "If you look at any president of the United States, you will find somebody who has an incredible list of personal and professional contacts." Essentially, they spent their career in politics building their network. This is true of anybody who reaches the top of their field in any profession, not just politics. If you look at anybody who is at the top, know that they didn't get there alone. They had a large list of contacts who helped them get to the top of their field.

And creating this large network comes from years of cultivating relationships. So follow-up is really the most important part of everything we're talking about. How many of you regularly send some sort of correspondence to people you meet in the business setting, when you meet them for the first time? How many of you regularly send some sort of follow-up? I see a few hands up in the audience. How many of you do it all the time, not just on occasion? Now there are fewer hands in the air. How many send handwritten notes for such follow-up? Not email. Wow, no hands left.

Many in this audience are technologists, so you live on email, thus this is not surprising. Email is not a bad thing; it just has become very common. I communicate by email all day long. But for a first follow-up, sending a handwritten note really stands out. And I know first-hand because I get 150 emails a day between my job, the book and speaking career, and the personal account my wife and I use at home. If somebody sent me an email and said, "Hey it was nice to meet you," I'd be touched and maybe thrilled that I made an impression. And then I would hit "delete." But if someone sends me a handwritten note, it is more experiential. It's more of an experience to actually receive an envelope, open it up, and read it. And then what do most people do? Most people don't put it right in the trash. They'll put it back on their desk and it sits there for a couple of days. I was doing this presentation for the sales team of a large newspaper when one of the sales guys whom I knew gets up and leaves the room—I thought he had an appointment and was leaving. He comes back two minutes later and throws a card down on the desk and says, "I received this from Thom three years ago when I first started this job and met him for the first time. It's been in my desk drawer ever since. It's the only handwritten note I've ever received after meeting someone new at a networking event." People sometimes put them in a drawer, and because they're not getting billions of notes, they never clean out that drawer. And every time they see it, they think, "Oh, yeah. I remember that guy." And maybe over time, you build a friendship. So I think you really stand out and you're really remembered if you take the time to do something a little bit different.

I'm not talking about writing a novel. It's just a couple of sentences acknowledging where you met, what you talked about, and the next step. "Hey, let's have lunch. I'll call you in a couple of weeks." Or something as simple as "Hey, let me know if I can help you out." When my wife and I got married, we had to write the thank-you notes, and we split the list. She said, "Here, you take your family and friends; I'll take my family and friends." I was done fairly quickly. Three weeks later, she's on thank-you note number nine. I asked, "What are you doing?" She was writing a page and a half to every person. It was long and included too much information for a short note.

She inquired, "Well what did **you** write in your notes?"

"I don't know. Short stuff."

"What did you say to your Aunt Catherine?"

"Dear Catherine, sorry you couldn't make the wedding. Thanks for the china place setting. Enclosed is a photo from our big day. Love, Thom and Sara."

"Well what did you say to your cousin Mary?" She's Catherine's daughter.

"Dear Mary, good to see you at the wedding. Thanks for the Waterford Crystal vase. Enclosed is a photo from our big day. Love, Thom and Sara."

My wife replies, "What if they compare notes?"

Yikes, I don't think they compared the notes. I am even more sure that people you send business correspondence to are not going to compare your letters!

People are always saying, "Well what if I meet two people from the same company? Do I have to personalize then?" Yes. Make the notes personal, but you do not have to make them long. They're not going to run down to the office and go, "Hey, did the guy who paid us a sales call write you? Look what he sent me." And if they do, they're not going to discredit you because you wrote a similar note. So keep it short and simple, but it does definitely stand out when you're able to do that.

You're going to meet people at these types of events, and there are a couple of things that you need to do. One is, send that follow-up, because just meeting them only makes them someone you've met. By doing some sort of follow-up, you make it more personal and you stand out in their mind. That email or that handwritten note is a second touch that you're making. So you send that short note.

You want to include your business card when you're sending that handwritten note. A lot of people will tell me, "Thom, I just met them. I gave them my business card last night. Why am I going to send another one?" Well, what do you think happens to the business cards when people go home? They take them out of their pockets; they put them next to the phone. Then they go to the office the next day. By sending a note with your card in it, you are getting your business contact information directly into their hands at their office so that they can put it into their database. You can't actually go and put it in their database for them, but you've done everything you can to give them that opportunity to have your contact information in the future.

If the person you met is a potential client, you want to put him or her in your database. You want to share with other people in your group. Do not make the mistake of keeping your networking connections secret from your co-workers. You should regularly share information with each other about whom you have met in your business community. Maybe someone else is trying to get into that company and now you can strategize that you know two different people, and now you have two ways to get into that company.

Beyond the Business Card

A business card alone isn't enough. You need to create a profile on the people you meet. You should create a history that records any items that you have talked about and unique facts that you have learned about the other person. What is important to them and what do they view as important for their career? What local charities do they support? What are their hobbies? Where do they like to vacation? Find out where they went to college or other important affiliations. Maybe that information could come in handy in the future—if their alma mater is coming to play basketball at a college near you and your company has season tickets, you would want to know who in your database attended the visiting college. If Duke University is playing in your city you could bring anyone who enjoys basketball. However, if you bring an alumnus from Duke they will appreciate the invitation even more. You need to gather and categorize the little tidbits of information about people so that you can make informed decisions about how to interact with those in your network.

Learn about their family. A lot of people say, "Well, I don't like to mix business and family. I don't ever talk about family with those in the business community. I keep it separate." I don't think that people compartmentalize the different parts of their lives as much as others think. I believe that all the parts of our lives interconnect. If I were to select a person from the audience and ask them about their children, I would imagine we would have a long conversation, as they would share with me many details of their kids' latest accomplishments. I've never once had somebody go, "No, I don't talk about my kids."

The idea is to get them talking about their life. Be on the lookout for things you have in common so that you can expand the discussion. If you also have kids you should inquire about the activities their family participates in. How old are their kids, etc. Well, maybe they play soccer or they are expert skiers. Maybe they play music, maybe they're a runner; there are all these types of different things that they may do for fun.

If someone tells me that they have a son or daughter that is in the martial arts, I would then have them for a longer conversation because my daughter has earned her black belt in karate. The point here is that we would have established a common link that we share. This is how people build relationships. They uncover points of interest that they have in common.

Helping Others Succeed

You should regularly look at your own network, the people you already know and those you have recently met. Whom do you know in your network who maybe could be their client, who maybe could help them? Be a connector and make regular introductions to others who could be beneficial contacts to one another. Maybe they have a special need and you know somebody who can solve that problem. Put people together even if there's nothing in it for you. Be on the lookout when you meet people for what's important for them. Then think about, "Whom do I already know that I can put together with them?"

Thinking first about others is the best way to get others to think about you. If you make it a point to help others succeed, then people will want to be part of your circle of influence. They will search out ways to make sure that you know they exist, and the smart ones will seek out ways to help you succeed first. Networking is NOT about an equal give and take, but the old saying "what goes around comes around" holds true for those who embrace the power of business relationships.

Be Creative

You should strive for ways to be creative in how you interact with your network. Many people think that sending a holiday card is the greatest marketing thing they can do to keep in constant contact with others. The only problem is, the prospective clients get hundreds of these holiday cards. They have no idea if you sent it or not. I'm not saying that you should not send holiday cards. But I am saying that it is not a unique way to stand out from your competition. Remember that many business professionals get hundreds of holiday cards, and they all are pretty much the same. I received around 150 such cards last year, and I could not begin to remember who sent them off the top of my head. The effort you put into holiday cards could be better served by sending them at a different time of year. In the last few years I have seen a few companies send their annual card at Thanksgiving, thus beating the traditional rush. I also have a friend, Susan Baughman, who annually sends St. Patrick's Day cards to all of her personal and professional friends. It stands out, as it is unique.

You need to out-think your competition every day. Be aware of what your competitors are doing in regards to their marketing and business development efforts. Then actively do something else. I have a friend who calls this "180 Degree Marketing." He looks around his industry and sees where all his competitors are going. What are they sponsoring? What are they doing with their clients? Where are they advertising? He goes 180 degrees the other way. He looks for unique ways to put himself in front of people, as unique is always remembered. He also finds that as soon as he is successful, three or four of his competitors are right there sponsoring that same event next time. He hosts a seminar, they host a seminar. He starts a blog, they start a blog. And so on, and so on. When that happens he goes and finds something else that is new and exciting. He doesn't want to be seen as a follower. Most companies do "me too marketing." Being average is a quick way to lose. It takes more effort to stand out and discover unique venues to get exposure, but winning is not easy. Nobody remembers companies or people who are average.

Be Confident

When it comes to networking and meeting people, a lot of people are just real shy. They're just real apprehensive about it. They think, "What do I bring to the table? Why would these people want to be talking to me?" You know what? You're smart, you're informed, and you work for one of the top companies in your industry. Other people come to the networking event with the desire to meet people too. They already want to talk to you. You bring a lot to the table, so you must embrace the confidence that you are just as important to them as they are to you. You don't want to be cocky; you want to be confident. There is a big difference.

Online Social Networking

In the last few years the Internet has taken hold of many aspects of our lives. Some of the main questions I get when I speak to audiences are inquiries about social online networking sites like LinkedIn, Facebook, MySpace, Plaxo, Twitter, and countless other communities that have popped up.

A few years ago I would have told you that these were great tools that were optional for you to use if you were so inclined. However, times have changed. Now I think that having an up-to-date and active online persona is a must if you are going to succeed in most industries.

The Internet allows others to take shortcuts in learning about you, your company, and your history. Our society is moving to be much more transparent, and while you do not, and should not, have all your information available on the Internet, having your résumé on a site like LinkedIn is now expected.

For business purposes I recommend LinkedIn, and have not found any reason not to have a profile on this site. More than ever, your prospects, clients, vendors, and others are going to this tool before a meeting to be able to better understand who you are and to look for ways to find connection points. If they cannot find you they do not say "oh well" or assume you have a good reason for not being present, but instead many just assume you are out of touch.

This is especially important if you are doing business with people who are under forty years old. The younger generations are very comfortable having their lives visible online. The flip side is that people need to be conscious of what they put out there. Too many younger professionals are discovering the downside of having their employers finding embarrassing photos or other information posted on more social-oriented websites such as MySpace or Facebook. The best advice is to not put anything online that you would not want your grandmother to hear about.

How to Make Your Network Work for You

Now that you have gone out and you've met all these people and you say, "Hey, this Thom Singer guy is onto something. I agree with everything he teaches. I'm going to do all of it. I am going to network like crazy." And you do, and you make many new contacts. Are you done? Nope. There's no end to networking. It does not stop, because it is part of a lifestyle. You have to maintain these relationships that you've been working on. You have to continue to send notes and emails and make phone calls to the people in your life. You have to continuously show them that they are important. If someone gets promoted or if something good happens for them, you need to honor their accomplishments. You need to celebrate the things that matter in their life. When people have a birthday, an anniversary, a wedding, you want to acknowledge it. Good things happen all the time in the lives of people we know. Celebrating with them helps build the bond that leads to more solid, ongoing, mutually beneficial relationships.

But you know what? The world is not always joyous. You've also got to support people when they're down. And this is hard because sometimes in our society when people are going through a rough time it is natural to shy away. Give them space. When someone loses a job, or misses a promotion, has a parent or spouse pass away, or, God forbid, an illness with one of their kids, they are in need of the support of friends. But in the business world we see people often pull away from those they know who are in sorrow. Do not avoid those in need of kind words or your compassion. Be the person who goes up to them and says, "Hey, sorry to hear you're having rough times."

My younger daughter was born with a condition where the bones in her skull were fused together. As she got older, as her brain grew, it was pushing out in different directions. And it was starting to become a real noticeable deformity when the doctors diagnosed the problem. I share this story for two reasons. Number one was, there were a lot of people who just hid when they saw me because it was a scary situation to have a child so young who would need such massive corrective surgery, and they didn't know what to say. But there were other people who came out of the woodwork to say, "Hey, is there anything we can do?" "Hey, I heard you're having a rough time." There were people who I barely knew from the business community who said, "I fly on Southwest Airlines so often, I've got all these free tickets. Can I give you free tickets so that your wife and your child and you can fly to the specialists that you have to see and it won't cost you anything?" It was the people who reached out to me and my family that forever will be remembered. Those who helped ease the fear with a smile will never be forgotten.

One person from my network called in the middle of the night—around two in the morning. I didn't even hear the phone—he must have called 16 times. I woke up and the answering machine was just blinking like mad. And he said, "Pick up the phone. Call me back. Pick up the phone." I called him back in the morning and he said, "I'm sorry to bother you, but I was talking to my cousin. He's a pediatric neurosurgeon." I told him, "Oh, we have already spoken with several doctors." The fix for this problem was they needed to remove her entire skull—the whole top of her skull was to be taken out.

He had reached out to his cousin to make sure we knew all the right questions to ask our doctors, but it turned out that his cousin was one of the top doctors in the country in treating the condition our daughter had. The cousin had pioneered a new way to do this surgery so that instead of two weeks in the hospital, she would be there three days. Instead of two full blood transfusions, she would have no blood transfusions during her surgery. This person went out of his way to get in contact with his cousin, who's one of the top pediatric neurosurgeons in the country, to not only take our call, but to treat us like part of his extended family. My wife and daughter ended up flying to San Diego two days later. It was because of our network that we found the doctor that saved Kate's life and gave her a full chance at a full life and a full recovery. Today Kate is fine, but at the time we were very scared. Having such a connection via a friend to our surgeon helped us through the situation.

Be that person who reaches out to help ease the pain of others. Maybe your cousin can't solve their problem, but maybe he can. Don't shy away when you see people having a rough time. Be the one who says, "Hey is there anything I can do?" Or, "Let me give you that plane ticket." Or, heck, "I'll say a prayer or I'll send good thoughts your way." I will never in my life forget any of those people who spoke up and offered a shoulder to lean on. A lot of those who made a difference were not close friends; instead they were traditional business acquaintances. Yet they did not turn away when they witnessed need. How wonderful to be that type of person. I will never forget any of them who reached out.

Another story that stands out in my mind about the day of my daughter's surgery was the delivery of a giant cookie bouquet—you've never seen so many cookies in your entire life. Now, Kate was only six months old and had just had her skull rebuilt, so these were not for her. They were for my wife, my five-year-old, and me! We ate them all in a matter of minutes. They were sent by the staff of a major venture capital firm with whom my boss did a lot of work. They didn't even know me that well, but we had worked together on several marketing projects in the technology industry. The venture firm's marketing manager was my friend and she and her bosses decided they wanted to do something, anything, to help my family. So they reached out and sent those cookies. I'll tell you what, I will never forget those little things that people did. The cookies probably cost them $60 and I'll never forget it. Be that person.

Reconnect

Throughout your life, you've had people in your business life and your personal life who've been a wonderful influence on your career and part of your network, but with whom you've lost touch. You know, college roommates, former bosses, former co-workers, people you went through training with at your first job. Where did those people go? It's so much easier to reconnect with an old friend and build that relationship than it is to start fresh with someone you just met today. Reach out to people you've lost touch with and bring them back into the fold, especially if they're in your industry and you've just drifted apart. Send them a note regularly after you've reconnected so you don't lose touch again. Use social media tools to make sure that you keep the connection alive and beneficial to both of you. You never know who is the next person who refers you business or brings you an amazing opportunity.

I gave this talk one time and someone from the audience came up to me and said, "You know, I had this roommate for two years in business school. We kind of had a falling out when we graduated, over the deposit on the apartment we shared near the university. I haven't spoken to him in six years. But when you said that part about reconnecting, I thought of him." Most people can quickly think of someone like that whom they have lost touch with. This person said he had always missed his former roommate, and wished the friendship had not ended. He asked me, "Do you think I can call him?" And I said, "Why not?" He said, "I don't even remember who was at fault for losing that deposit." I encouraged him to make the call that day.

I got a note from him a couple of weeks later and he said he had searched for his former friend on the Internet and found him on LinkedIn. Although he had moved away from the city where they lived after graduate school, he was now living back in town. His friend was happy to hear from him and they decided to meet for lunch. Both were thrilled to put the past behind them and start fresh. All it took to reconnect was a phone call.

If you just thought of someone from your past with whom you drifted apart, take the action this week of reaching out. Will they be glad to hear from you? Maybe. What if they called you tomorrow? Would you be happy? If yes, then get off your seat and make the call. Be the person that takes the initiative.

Have a Plan

With networking, as with any part of your life, you have to have a plan. If you were going to get on a plane today in Los Angeles and fly to Honolulu, Hawaii, you would trust that your pilot would have to have a plan. One would not want a pilot to simply take off and climb to 50,000 feet and just "head west." If that happened you might reach your destination. But if you have ever seen a map of the Pacific Ocean you know that there's a lot of blue between L.A. and Honolulu. You would want your pilot to have a plan if he was going to fly you to your destination. The same thing is true with building your network. Have a plan.

What types of individuals or companies do you prefer to do business with? Who can refer business to you? What types of people make the best clients? It's different for everyone, so I cannot hand you a template for your plan. There would be a different plan for each person in the audience. You need to examine your own situation and understand whom you need to know. You also need to know whom you can help. If you approach networking as only being about seeking out those who can help you, then you are destined to fail.

Know who are your top five people in your industry that you want to know. Maybe it's someone you would hope could be a client, or maybe someone who could be a wonderful referral source. Maybe it's someone you just admire. Who is it that you want to know in the business world? If you have never thought about this, you should. Having a clear idea of the individuals or the types of individuals that you desire to add to your network will make it much easier for you to find them.

Look to the long term in your career. Do you have a mentor? Is there someone in your industry, inside your company or out, whom you admire? Look at what they've done. How did they build their network? How did they grow their career? Find them and ask them how they accomplished their success. Let them know that you desire to make the same type of career path for yourself. Inquire if they would be willing to mentor you. If you make the effort, you'd be surprised how many people will open up their lives to you and share with you and help you and introduce you to people inside their Rolodex.

Internal Networking

Internal networking is equally as important to your success. Networking should not only be limited to trying to find new sales. It's not just for referral sources. Look inside your company for people with whom you can forge long-term, mutually beneficial relationships, as promotions most often go to those who have created positive internal brands inside the organization. Those who are the best networked inside a company are the ones who excel. Everything we've talked about thus far works the same way inside the company as it does outside the company. When others move on or move up in the company, they often bring other people in their network with them to that new job, to that new role, to that new team.

It is people in our lives that help us reach our goals. When there are tough sales cycles, when there are tough things in the economy, it's the allies that you have inside the company that help you stay secure. And you never know who will rise up to one day become the CEO of your company or another company. You never know who might be the person who can most benefit your career—not tonight, not next week, but maybe five, ten years from now. You don't know, so you must make it a practice of treating everyone with respect if you want exciting opportunities to come your way. And if you don't have those internal connections, you're missing the boat on your future.

The Networking Quotient

So how are you doing? How do you compare to your peers? What's your networking quotient? How do you compare to other people when it comes to building relationships in your business that can help you succeed? Well, I'm going to ask you all to do something. I'm going to ask you all to go to www.thomsinger.com. Or you can go to networkingquotient.com, but it might be easier just to remember my name.

Go to www.thomsinger.com and there's a free online quiz. It's 30 questions and it only takes eight minutes to complete. You put in a couple of pieces of demographic information, and immediately after you take the quiz, you will receive your rank based on the skills we discussed in this presentation. The quiz is all about how you react in a variety of networking situations. But it is not about getting the best score. Instead it is about thinking about the reasons for the questions. Maybe you're already doing great when it comes to building relationships with people in your industry. Maybe you need some work. It will assist you in thinking about ways to improve and how to embrace the power of business relationships.

The quiz will also show you how you compare to other people in your industry who have taken the quiz. It will give you a break-out of all the demographics that you entered amongst men, amongst women, amongst people in your income level and industry. It'll break it all down to that level and show you areas to improve.

About The Author

Thom Singer has two decades of marketing and business development experience with firms such as RR Donnelley, Brobeck Phleger & Harrison LLP, Marsh, Inc., and Wells Fargo Bank. He has trained over 10,000 thousand professionals in the art of building contacts that lead to increased business. He is an expert in branding, positioning, and networking, and has trained over 10,000 professionals in the art of building professional contacts that lead to increased business.

Thom has authored five books on the power of business relationships and networking, and is an engaging professional speaker. He has addressed audiences as large as 1,500 and encourages everyone to embrace and cultivate their network while helping others succeed.

Thom and his wife, Sara, make their home in Austin, Texas and are the parents of two highly-spirited daughters.

He can be emailed at thom@thomsinger.com
www.thomsinger.com